Nāgārjuna's Tree of Wisdom
A Translation

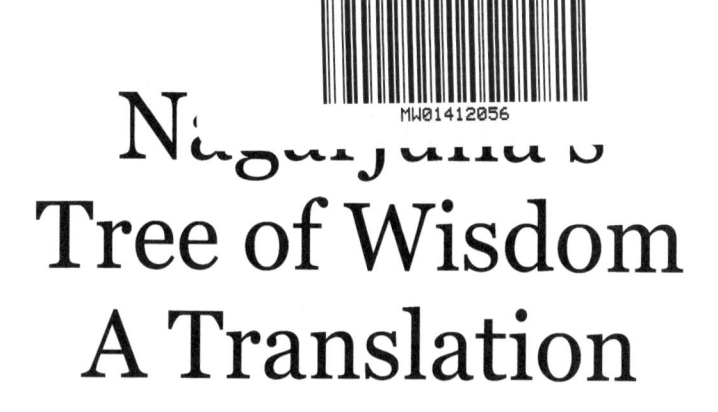

Dennis Waller
A Tibetan Buddhist Text

Edited by Martin Ash

Copyright © 2012 Dennis Waller

All rights reserved.

ISBN: 1481169025
ISBN-13: 978-1481169028

DEDICATION

To

Jennifer LaBarba McLochlin

For her friendship and support

CONTENTS

	Acknowledgments	i
1	What is the Tree of Wisdom	1
2	Who is Nagarjuna	5
3	A Translation	9
4	Conviction of the Heart	85
	About the Author	95

ACKNOWLEDGMENTS

For the work of W. L. Campbell for bringing the Tree of Wisdom into English for the first time in 1918.

And to Martin Ash for his contribution in editing.

CHAPTER ONE
WHAT IS THE TREE OF WISDOM

The Tree of Wisdom by Nagarjuna is a treatise on morals and ethics written over 2,000 years ago. This commentary on moral living is very similar to other text such as the Tao Te Ching by Lao Tzu, the Hsin Hsin Ming by Seng Ts'an, the Enchiridion by Epictetus, and Meditations by Marcus Aurelius.

It's remarkable that this is only the second English translation of this ancient text from this incredible Indian philosopher. The first translation into English was done by W.L. Campbell in 1918. At the time of Campbell's translation, there was so much already lost to history in the allegories that the meaning couldn't be extrapolated for all the verses.

This version has been interpreted into a more modern new age style yet it still possesses the essence of the message that Nagarjuna implied. I prefer to use the word interpretation over the word translation as this is more of a rendering constructed to clarify the meaning in such a way that it is easy to grasp the concepts. However, there are a few verses that have been left in the original Campbell translation as their relevance hasn't changed.

The primary difference between the Tree of Wisdom and the Tao Te Ching is the Tree of Wisdom takes a more "matter of fact" practical approach to life where the Tao Te Ching is more spiritual and esoteric. Both have the same basic underlying principles, they are just different paths to the same goal.

The Tree of Wisdom is made up of 260 verses containing just over 8,000 words. In the tradition of Buddhism, there are a few verses that will leave you confused. This is natural as in the contemplation of the verse, the understanding will become clear.

One major difference in this translation and Campbell's is the use of the way. Where the word "way" is used, it is to imply the way of the Tao Te Ching. I encourage those who are not familiar with the Tao Te Ching to read it as the two text complement each other.

To illustrate the concept of the Tree of Wisdom, here are a two of the verses within the text that convey the universal nature of the teachings of Nagarjuna. "Strive to have your accomplishments serve others, rather than have them serve your ego. If ego rules your actions, then how are morals attained?" and " Live life free of the fear of the unknown, for there is nothing to fear. Live life free of the fear of the known, for you can conquer those fears."

If all you did was just apply these two principles to your daily life, could you imagine the possibilities of the significant change that could take place in your life? Just overcoming your fears and living the life you truly desire and know that your actions are not only benefiting but others, wouldn't that be incredible? That would be change beyond measure. Now, just imagine if you applied more than just two verses to your life? Imagine immersing yourself into the wholeness of the text, what would your life be like? There is a whole new world waiting for you, all that is required is your willingness to get up and get going.

CHAPTER TWO
WHO IS NAGARJUNA

Nagarjuna was an Indian philosopher who lived around 150 to 250AD. He is credited with being the founder of the "Middle Path" (Madhyamaka) in the Buddhist school of the Mahayana Tradition. Nagarjuna is considered among scholars to be the most influential thinker after Gautama Buddha within Buddhism. As a matter of fact, Nagarjuna is considered to be the second Buddha among Tibetan and East Asian traditions of Buddhism.

There are several texts and treatises attributed to Nagarjuna including the treatise on Rasayana Alchemy, and many sutras such as the 70 verses on Emptiness, and Requisites of Enlightenment. Another important note is Nagarjuna is considered the one to have introduced the concept of "emptiness" to Buddhism. He also understood the dynamics of duality in that of existence and non-existence. He taught the concept of relativity in that our experiences are all comparative to our perception. There is only long because short exists, however what may be long to you might be short to someone else. He believed that one should strive for non-dualistic wisdom and compassion while living in a dualistic world. Within his teachings is the underlying message to live life in accordance with the laws of nature. Amazing that he was able to keep a common sense approach to his work that is easy to grasp. Even more amazing, his principles are strangely similar to the principles of Quantum Physics. This is remarkable considering that he lived about 1,800 years before the birth of Quantum Physics.

Like all Mystical Sages in Buddhism, little is known about the history of Nagarjuna. In the same tradition as Lao Tzu and Seng Ts'an, Nagarjuna's legend has become mythical. There are stories of Nagarjuna learning alchemy. It is said in legend that he used this lost art to transmute lead into gold to supply the Nalanda monks of the Nalanda Monastic University in northern India during a time of famine. There are several stories of Nagarjuna. One where he defeated 500 non-

Buddhists in a debate.

Another story and perhaps the most fantastic is the story of his death. It is said that the life span of Nagarjuna was attached to the King Udayibhadra. This king had a son, Kumara Shaktiman and he wanted to be the king. The wife of the king and Kumara's mother, had instructed Kumara that in order to become king, he would need to cut Nagarjuna's head off. The mother also said that since Nagarjuna is such a compassionate man that surely he would agree.

Amazingly, Nagarjuna agreed. However Kumara couldn't cut off his head with a sword. Nagarjuna said that in a previous life he had killed an ant while cutting grass. Therefore, due to karma, only the blade of kusha grass could cut Nagarjuna. Kumara did this and was able to behead Nagarjuna. Strangely enough upon his supposed death, the blood coming from the severed head turned into milk and the head spoke, " Now, I will go to Sukhavati but I will enter this body once again." Sukhavati is the western pure land of the Buddha Amitabha. Sukhavati translates to mean, "Land of Bliss" Upon this revelation from the talking head, Kumara separated the head from the body as far as possible. However, legend states that every year the head and body become closer and closer to each other. When the head joins with the body, it is said that Nagarjuna will return to this world to walk again.

What is amazing about Nagarjuna besides the legends and writings, is while he is considered one of the most influential members of Buddhism, he is almost unknown outside the circles of Buddhism. I was shocked and surprised to see this text so obscure in today's world. I hope by bringing this ancient text to life again, the teachings of Nagarjuna will become as popular and well known as Lao Tzu's Tao Te Ching or Epictetus's Enchiridion.

CHAPTER THREE
A TRANSLATION

verse 1-

Evil people should be dealt with and placed under control.
The wise should be held in reverence.
Quest to fill your soul with honest deeds,
And have compassion for your own countrymen

verse 2-

With regards to your own secrets and those of others,
Guard these as your own dear child.
For those for whom all earthly things are equal,
Will have love in their heart for all men.

verse 3-

If your wife is evil and your friend evil,
If the King is evil and your relatives evil,
If your neighbor is evil and the country evil,
Then abandon them and make haste for a distant land.

verse 4-

Avoid those who are greedy for wealth.
Avoid a wife who is fond of fornication.
Abandon these people and seek those of good morals.
Be with those who are strong and virtuous.

verse 5-

Although you know the difference between good and bad deeds,
You should carry out your actions after careful consideration.
Although you may only partially succeed,
You are to be admired for your purity of heart and mind.

verse 6-

The steadfast who speak with few words and politely,
Are very much respected and admired by their peers.
As the sun rises from the night and by his rays creates great heat,
You too should let your actions speak highly of you

verse 7-

Though you may suffer for your convictions in the face of adversity,
Be not anxious but steadfast in your heart and mind.
As surely as the sun has set for the night,
Will it not shine again in the morning?

verse 8-

As the gardener knows that it is mother earth that produces the flowers.
While flowers are admired and loved, they are fleeting.
Be not forgetful of the source of this beauty.
In the same way, you should be like the root firmly planted.

verse 9-

Do not ever compromise your morals and values for material gain,
Whether it is for royal favor or rewards.
For these are transitory and will vanish in time,
But a good heart that is pure will last indefinitely.

verse 10-

Things not understood are to be avoided till they are clear.
Be not indifferent to the concerns of health, liberty, or life.
Be not indifferent to your obligations.
Honor your obligations with due diligence.

verse 11-

Worthy men do not make many promises.
But when a promise is made,
It is made as if carved in stone,
And to be honored even at the cost of death.

verse 12-

On occasion you will agree with your foes for the time is right.
On occasion you'll disagree with your friends, and that time will be right.
Learn to distinguish when you should and should not agree.
The clever man will always seize opportunities when presented to him.

verse 13-

Be mindful of the words you speak.
For words spoken cannot be retracted.
Learn to accomplish through actions rather than speech.
Conquer through silence rather than through senseless noise.

verse 14-

Preparedness is necessary in order to keep adversaries at bay.
By being persistent at being prepared is to overcome.
Ignorance is to assume that all will be well.
This course of thought will result in being defeated.

verse 15-

Keep your thoughts to yourself as you would a secret,
Thoughts made public are prone to be defended.
Be strong and silent like the root.
For it is the flower that gets cut.

verse 16-

Although you may witness beyond the veil in this world.
Others cannot perceive past the veil.
Make no mention of this.
Rather you would welcomed being ridiculed.

verse 17-

Be wary of any wolf wrapped in sheep's clothing.
Know this disguise of evil well.
For this evil is presented within niceties.
Don't be brought to slaughter by a sweet song.

verse 18-

Impress upon others the thoughts you choose for them.
Have them contemplate your thoughts.
While believing that these thoughts are their own.
This is the key to controlling men.

verse 19-

Be humble in your ways.
Desire not the trappings of success.
For earthly wealth brings misery and quarrelling.
Life is easier being contented with little.

verse 20-

It is mankind's nature not to quarrel or war.
Wealth obtained by quarrelling will soon be fleeting.
Why would you choose to lose your soul for earthly wealth?
Earthy wealth is nothing more than an illusion.

verse 21-

The foolish are those who fill their plate with more than they can eat,
Those who continue to pour tea into their cup after it is filled,
Whose eyes are larger than their mind and make their thoughts public.
These four traits are a living death.

verse 22-

Give no respect or thought to those who are evil minded,
Not for a prince, not for deceitful family,
Not for an unfaithful woman,
For these are sinners who have cast their fate.

verse 23-

Hold no earthly attachments to your possessions.
For the man consumed with possessiveness will suffer.
Possessiveness and attachment bring with them greed.
Theses are traits of evil.

verse 24-

A man of much worldly knowledge has two forms of happiness.
Either he will renounce attachment to worldly possessions,
Or abandon all earthly interest.
Either way, he will experience true freedom.

verse 25-

When your glory has abandoned you,
And your efforts have become meaningless.
There is only one happiness for you.
By returning and becoming one with nature.

verse 26-

The life of a wise and holy man is like that of a flower.
Either to be admired by the masses.
Or to be lost to the world.
Like the flower on the forest floor.

verse 27-

Life that perishes naturally is a life that ends modestly.
As so you should live, with a sense of moderation.
For living with moderation has its essence.
Especially if your intellect is not developed.

verse 28-

This is the thing to understand.
The Law of Familiarity.
Don't be too vocal or visual for this diminishes fear within others.
The master knows the importance of balance of caring and not.

verse 29-

Like the moon from waxing to fullness,
Like the bees making honey,
Like the possessions of the wealthy
Abundance comes from gradual accumulation.

verse 30-

Do not be excessively covetous or envious.
When consumed with these desires,
Pain and sorrow will surely follow.
For this is the punishment of such actions.

verse 31-

Ensure you can protect the wealth you have conquered,
Before going forward in acquiring more acquisitions.
Don't be overcome by greed or lust for more.
This action will result in the theft of your possessions by your neighbor.

verse 32-

Do not covet fame for it is hollow in its wisdom and knowledge.
Be honest in judging yourself.
Desires for such fame will take you off the path.
Such fame will take you from your purpose.

verse 33-

Do not say things which will bring pain to others.
Know that words are like swords that cut deeply.
The word and sword are known as equals throughout the lands,
And can equally kill in one stroke.

verse 34-

Be wary of sweet gifts of your enemy.
Don't be overcome by outward beauty.
The wise look at the essence of the gift before accepting.
Adhering to this principle will avoid injury.

verse 35-

To the benefit of your enemy, be just in your intentions.
Be guided by reason and truth in a compassionate manner
Then see your enemies come to you with their hands folded
And bow to you in devotion.

verse 36-

Injure your enemy by kindness rather than conflict.
Praise his good qualities and strengths.
Know that whatever harm you hold within,
Will injure you and not your enemy.

verse 37-

Be steadfast in dealing with those who don't conform.
Use harsh measures if necessary.
Be like a father to his own children.
Does not the father threaten punishment against infractions?

verse 38-

As long as you stay on the path of the Way,
As long as your steps are steady with commitment,
As long as your wisdom is unimpaired,
Your rewards will be beyond measure.

verse 39-

Be free from what is expected of you by the masses.
To do this is to be free from them.
Don't try to please everyone as this is impossible.
Choose to honor yourself to have peace.

verse 40-

For the fool seeks what he doesn't know,
Desires what he has no knowledge of,
Bursting with pride while having no substance,
For these traits make a fool.

verse 41-

Be careful who you befriend.
Like the wind was befriended by the fire,
It was the wind that brought death to the fire.
Likewise weak men create their demise by the friends they choose.

verse 42-

Choose to do no harm to others,
Choose not to let low people rule you.
Choose to stay on the path of virtue.
Choose not to abandon this principle.

verse 43-

Living a day in the Divine Love of the Way,
Is greater than living a hundred years in worldly ways.
Live not the ways of the world,
Strive to live in the way of the Way.

verse 44-

When the weak minded come into wealth,
They become consumed with greed and pride.
When the virtuous attain wealth,
They remain humble as the poor.

verse 45-

Worldly people are like lowly forms of life.
Quarreling rules their days,
Their greed blinds their sight,
Peace is ever eluding.

verse 46-

When worldly people possess wealth,
They become boastful and proud.
The wise on the other hand stay steadfast,
Even with wealth, they remain humble.

verse 47-

The virtuous don't engage in quarreling, nor being prideful.
The virtuous don't use foul language, nor covet the flesh,
Nor do they work without profit
These are the not traits of the virtuous.

verse 48-

Those consumed by pride would rather suffer,
Than to admit being in need of assistance.
In order to maintain outwardly appearances,
Suffering is preferred rather than to succumb to asking for help.

verse 49-

There is a bird which lives off the morning dew.
For it fears the imprisonment of obligation.
To have no obligation to anyone,
Is to have your freedom.

verse 50-

The enlightened have no need for a teacher.
As the cured have no need for a doctor.
Once the water is crossed, there is no need of the ferry.
Once a task is complete, there is no need to do it again.

verse 51-

Even an evil man, weak and in good nature,
Can be dealt with easily.
And like calm waters,
He shouldn't be disturbed.

verse 52-

When people become unyielding in their beliefs,
And confrontations arise,
There will be no ground for compromise.
How can this be of any benefit to anyone?

verse 53-

When ego rules the conversation,
Expect the discussion to be boisterous,
By men filled with pride and arrogance.
That gathering will bear no fruit.

verse 54-

Addictions rob the body, mind and soul of peace.
Stay clear of such behavior.
For it unsettles the mind
And takes strength from the body.

verse 55-

The man filled with greed and selfishness,
Is like a barking dog with no bite.
He is of no benefit to anyone,
Therefore, what is his purpose.

verse 56-

In times of misfortune, whether it is natural or by war,
In times of distress, all are equal alike,
A time of famine or danger from enemies,
The king and the impoverished are affected the same.

verse 57-

People consumed with greed are never satisfied,
They continue to strive for worldly possessions.
This is not natural, for even a calf exhausting the milk,
Will leave the mother cow and go to a distance.

verse 58-

Losing one's affection, the contempt of one's own people,
To be much in debt, to be accused of wrongdoings,
To be abandoned by friends who see your poverty,
These five are not fire yet they burn the body the same.

verse 59-

Address problems as soon as they are born.
Do not allow them to mature.
As they are easy to defeat in infancy,
They are hard to overcome at maturity.

verse 60-

He who has knowledge is firm and steadfast.
The wise, even when destitute, keep to their virtues.
Like the scorching heat of the sun,
The natural coldness of the snow remains.

verse 61-

Those who live in the Way live forever.
Those who live in the flesh, die in the flesh.
Those who are self-absorbed and live in conceit,
Are already bound in damnation.

verse 62-

Those who live in the desire of sin are blind to the Way.
As the blind cannot see the beauty of a sunset,
Neither can the self-absorbed and greedy see the Way.
Living in ego blinds one from seeing the real truth.

verse 63-

The subtle ways of water, the creeping vine,
Turtles, and crafty women are the ways of,
Small distinctions that bring success.
For these subtle ways overcome adversity.

verse 64-

What goes around comes around,
Like misery follows pleasure,
And pleasure follows misery.
This too will pass like the night into day.

verse 65-

Things come and go throughout life
Make no attachments to any of them.
With attachment comes pain and suffering
Know that it is all an illusion.

verse 66-

As the sun rises and sits,
So we will be born and die
Have comfort in knowing this truth,
That your essence is not affected by these actions.

verse 67-

The angry are defeated before the battle begins.
Evil is brought upon evil by their actions.
While the fool confronts evil with anger,
The wise conquers by not being angry.

verse 68-

As a large stone can be rolled down the hill with little force,
So can your ego be affected by the smallest distinction.
By like a big oak tree,
Firmly planted in the ground.

verse 69-

Leave be those things that are to be left alone.
For engaging in these affairs will only bring grief.
Like that of trying to grasp the clouds.
Concern yourself with your own matters.

verse 70-

The man who meddles in the affairs of others,
Will have despair as his guest in the evening.
He that finds comfort in the misery of others,
Will surely be brought down.

verse 71-

What does it benefit a man to know the affairs of his neighbors,
While his own home is in disarray?
Like the cat that is watched by the dog,
The mouse is free to roam.

verse 72-

Thoughts become clear in a still mind
Like the reflection of the moon on a calm pond.
Clarity comes to the stillness.
Practice stillness to know inner truth.

verse 73-

A mouse who undertakes any task,
Whether it is large or small,
With the intent of doing his best work,
Will be met with the respect of the lion.

verse 74-

Many have met their death on assumption.
At all times be certain of your actions.
Rely not on others for your well being.
Be vigilant of your thoughts.

verse 75-

The man who acts out of love and compassion,
Will be met with great success.
One who lives in unconditional love,
Will surely control his own fate.

verse 76-

By always uttering pleasant speeches,
It is easy for a king to beguile his people.
However meaningful words should have value like gold,
Speak these words with the same rarity as gold.

verse 77-

Follow your own intuition.
Even when it is not popular among others.
Stay true to your truth.
Even when confronted with those who appear more wise than you.

verse 78-

He that knows the power within his wealth and ability,
Will prove to be a formidable foe,
One to be avoided at all cost.
His wrath is such that it has no equal.

verse 79-

If fire can burn in water,
Then what can extinguish it?
Fear born from within is like this fire.
Protect yourself from fear and cast it out.

verse 80-

Even a drum when not properly tuned will produce ill sounds.
Treat your world like a finely tuned drum to ensure sweet sounds.
Be aware of this to preserve tranquility and peace.
Not only for you but for those around you

verse 81-

Those who are self absorbed and greedy,
Know not the distinction between causing pain and joy.
All that matters are their own concerns,
At the cost of others, is not their worry.

verse 82-

It is better to give freely what can be given,
Rather risk loss of life and liberty.
Like the sheep that have their fleece sheared,
The essence of the sheep remain and the fleece will return.

verse 83-

When there is a snake at the root and an eagle above,
Monkeys climbing in the branches and the flowers surrounded by bees,
A resting place is provided for all of nature's animals,
Know that nature provides for all within its domain.

verse 84-

In battles of war,
It is not the physical aspects that win,
Rather it is the mental aspects that bring victory,
Cunning and cleverness rule over brute strength.

verse 85-

Strength without cunning is worthless,
Against an opponent that possesses cunning and cleverness.
He who understands this is mighty.
For even a lion can be brought down by a mouse.

verse 86-

Seek from those who possess the knowledge you desire.
A journey started is better than one never attempted.
Success is measured by the distance gained.
Not in hope and wishes.

verse 87-

The actions of the virtuous speak louder than words.
Words of worldly people bring no comfort.
Follow the example of the master.
This is the key for the student to learn.

verse 88-

Confront your fears head on with determination,
Rather than sulk in misery.
Take the necessary actions and control,
Thus fears are conquered.

verse 89-

Live life free of the fear of the unknown,
For there is nothing to fear.
Live life free of the fear of the known,
For you can conquer those fears.

verse 90-

Speak not of your cleverness to the deaf.
Show not your knowledge to the blind.
Comfort not those who do not seek comfort.
Give not your food to those who have no craving.

verse 91-

Resist the temptation to be proud,
Not in your youth, strength, or knowledge,
Not in riches, wealth, or health,
Be humble in your thoughts and actions.

verse 92

Whatever harm you cause, you bring to yourself.
Whether man or beast, bring no harm onto either.
To practice this principle is to be one with the way.
Therefore like the sun, burning brightly for all to see.

verse 93-

Speaking in lies and falsehoods,
Acting in an unbecoming manner,
Not heeding your nature,
These are the traits of a fool.

verse 94-

Seek to immerse yourself,
In that which is wise and holy.
By immersion you may become,
Wise and holy.

verse 95-

Choose your moments to speak,
For speaking at the right time ensures ,
That your words carry weight.
By treating your words like gold, others will treasure them.

verse 96-

Patience and perseverance,
Duty and honor,
Wisdom and courage,
Together bond a force that even the Gods fear.

verse 97-

Trust not your enemy, not even in defeat.
More kings have been defeated by betrayal.
Do not forget this principle,
Or your fate will be that of the hare served for dinner.

verse 98-

Bodily functions and desires are the same for the ignorant and the wise.
By the practice of the way, the ignorant can rise above.
If the way is not understood, the ignorant will remain in darkness.

verse 99-

The ignorant that speak ill of the way,
Are like day and night,
They come and go.
They may breathe but there is no life in them.

verse 100-

The ignorant that ignore the way,
Are like those dying of thirst,
While being next to a stream,
They struggle to dig a well with no avail.

verse 101-

Although you may remain on vacation for a very long time,
It is absolutely certain that you will have to return home.
Whatever may be the circumstances.
Returning home cannot be avoided.

verse 102-

Excessive pain is caused by attachment,
When separation isn't accepted,
But if it is voluntary by the act of letting go,
Infinite peaceful happiness will be obtained.

verse 103-

One's desire is to be attractive and happy,
And wealth is of course pleasant and natural.
But yet this world of existence,
Is but an illusion, temporary and fleeting.

verse 104-

Lust is the most detrimental of sins.
Envy is the most harmful to others.
Cunningness is a wolf in sheep's clothing.
But Generosity has no equal in its purity.

verse 105-

There is no light like the light of wisdom.
There is no darkness like that of spiritual darkness.
The blindness to the way is the worse of blindness.
Strive for the light of wisdom as wisdom has no equal.

verse 106-

As certain as the sun will rise tomorrow.
So too will death come to you.
With this knowing turn your mind from worldly thoughts,
And rejoice while on the path of the Way.

verse 107-

Desire for earthly jewels has been the downfall of many.
Temper your lust for these as their value is fleeting,
Rather desire for the jewels of the divine.
For these are the everlasting jewels of the Way.

verse 108-

The wise possess tranquility in abundance.
For they know that the riches of the earth,
Gold, cattle, grain, land, wealth, or health,
None of these can sustain the soul forever.

verse 109-

Hoarding wealth brings great pain and suffering,
In fears of it being stolen or lost.
While entertaining at times,
In the end it brings more misery than joy.

verse 110-

Nothing earthly is everlasting.
Strive to acquire what is everlasting.
Quest not to own earthly treasures,
Rather seek those treasures of the divine.

verse 111-

A king is never satisfied with great wealth.
A clever man is never fulfilled with hearing his words.
Never is there enough beauty in the world for these men.
These things are like the desires of a child, never satisfied.

verse 112-

Consume yourself with high morals and virtues.
Composure, self-reliance, control over your thoughts.
Whoever possesses these traits are contented,
For what more do they need.

verse 113-

If you are fully contented with your life,
You are far from the thoughts of evil.
Desires of carnal pleasure bring with them troubles.
This is the source of evil thoughts.

verse 114-

With all the faults of being human,
There remains one great moral quality.
And that is the power to choose,
Choose wisely.

verse 115-

Strive to attain modesty and contentment,
For these traits know not death.
Like the elephant, powerful as it may be,
Sustains on grass.

verse 116-

Is there really such a thing as personal property?
Does not the light of the sun belong to everyone?
Is not the air available for all to breathe?
What use then is this personal property?

verse 117-

The surest possession is real contentment.
It is not difficult to earn a living.
Like nature, there is an abundance throughout.
There is no place where it cannot be found.

verse 118-

Like nature where the tiger rules and the elephant is king.
Make your place among the grass and trees.
And eat the fruits of the trees.
The ways of evil men and society are not a real life.

verse 119-

The man that accepts his fate,
Whether good or bad,
And keeps his heart and mind pure,
Has no need of worldly wealth.

verse 120-

Your body is like a ship and your good actions,
Are the winds that sail the ship,
Over the ocean of human misery.
So long as your ship is not wrecked.

verse 121-

As long as the moon shines and sun rises,
And so long as death is on holiday,
Keep chaste in your actions,
And be pure of heart and mind.

verse 122-

Standing on the precipice of your death,
On watching the sunset on your life as you leave,
You'll make the journey alone as it should be.
A wife or child will be of no assistance on this journey.

verse 123-

The man who can rejoice with contentment,
Who can find happiness in simple things,
And who lives in concert with nature,
Upon discarding his body will have salvation.

verse 124-

If your thoughts are motivated by wisdom,
Then salvation is very near.
For salvation comes from within,
Not from wearing robes of ochre.

verse 125-

What does it avail a man to place clothes on his body?
Feed his stomach and neglect his heart and soul?
For the man that has the love of all living things,
In his heart and soul has no need of robes of ochre.

verse 126-

He who is quiet in the prime of life,
I know in order for this person to be quiet,
If all the senses were completely exhausted by age,
How could he possibly not be quiet?

verse 127-

As wood is transformed into smoke by the act of fire.
So too is your soul when awakened to the Way.
With this new change over you, strive to walk on the path,
And practice acts of virtue along your way.

verse 128-

Wealth, acquired through theft, mischievous means,
Or by acts not acceptable to the community,
Or by betrayal of your neighbors,
Such acquiring of wealth is not proper wealth.

verse 129-

Being concerned by what others think about you,
Will only bring misery, for this is vanity.
The man of virtue does not concern himself with such thoughts.
By not discriminating one or the other, this man is happier.

verse 130-

He that has no sense of right or wrong,
Or only concerns himself with himself,
Who quest to fulfill only his own desires,
What difference is there between this man and the beasts?

verse 131-

Knowledge is the great source of virtues.
Both visible and invisible therefore should be desired.
For to take hold of wisdom in its entirety,
Requires that you accept both visible and invisible.

verse 132-

One out of a hundred is born a hero.
One out of a thousand is born clever.
One out of hundred thousand is born wise.
But a wise hero may be born in one.

verse 133-

The wise never cease to quest to learn regardless of age,
Even though there may be no benefits of it in this life.
For this knowledge learned is not for naught,
As it will be available to them in another life.

verse 134-

Even one near death desiring to learn,
Should be treasured by others.
For he is like the empty tea cup,
His heart and mind is always open and able to receive.

verse 135-

Take a king and a wise man.
These two are not alike.
A king is respected in his own country,
While a wise man is respected everywhere.

verse 136-

Although the wise man has faults,
Philosophers will not grieve over this.
Like the moon that shines in its radiance,
View with pleasure regardless of its stains.

verse 137-

The ego attains great pleasure in accomplishments.
The ego attains great misery in mental worry.
Patience is the great protector of the mind.
Charity is the great protector of the soul.

verse 138-

Although the holy man may live far away,
His virtues act as a messenger and carry far.
Through sniffing the fragrance of the flowers,
The bees are attracted themselves.

verse 139-

If you are pretending to have virtue,
There is no use of your arrogant attitude.
Like the cow which has no milk,
Even if a bell be attached to it, will not be purchased.

verse 140-

While science knows much, our existence is short.
We estimate the length of life but we do not know for certain.
So, like the swan which separates milk from water,
Devote yourself to whatever you undertake.

verse 141-

Although there are many stars shining,
And the moon shines brightly too.
However when the sun sets it becomes night,
If not for the sun, there would be no east or west.

verse 142-

On whatever light shines on,
Darkness is chased away.
The shining of the sun being supreme,
What is there in the shining of the moon?

verse 143-

Like the moon, when full, outshines all the stars.
The man who accomplishes one single act thoroughly,
Surpasses all others who perform many acts.
Be as the moon, for the multitude of stars have not this power.

verse 144-

The growth of moral virtue depends on one's self.
The acquisition of property depends on previous merit.
Why blame anybody for this?
For this is the way of nature.

verse 145-

Moral virtues are obtained by making an effort,
And as this effort rests wholly within yourself,
To say that others possess moral virtues,
Is to see yourself in them.

verse 146-

Of those who understand the meaning of the scriptures,
There are many even among the crippled.
It is a matter for rejoicing to find the sharp-pointed sword,
By which the enemy is conquered.

verse 147-

There are rich men among the poor.
There are heroes among the cowards.
But the holy men who knows the way,
Are the rarest of all.

verse 148-

As there are no pearls to be found among elephants,
Or gold to be found growing on a tree.
The holy and wise that can point to the way,
Are not to be found everywhere.

verse 149-

Real Truth is a virtue to the enlightened.
But a harmful thing to those living in darkness.
The water of the river is very free from impurity;
But, entering the ocean, it becomes undrinkable.

verse 150-

The refined relish in refinement..
Barbarians have no use for refinement
Bees are attracted by the fragrance of flowers.
The frogs, although living together, are not.

verse 151-

The fame of those with keen discernment and sound judgment,
Are known among others with the same traits.
For they are as valuables among experts,
And heroes in battle.

verse 152-

The swan does not fit in well in the company of hawks.
Nor does a horse among the pigs,
Nor does a lion among the foxes,
Nor the clever man among fools.

verse 153-

Those who are acknowledged by the exulted,
Which upon their heads is placed a wreath,
May be considered vulgar by those,
Who are unworthy of such recognition.

verse 154-

Though possessing it, they don't proclaim it.
While others have it in small measure,
Holy men delight in such moral virtue.
How remarkable is such conduct!

verse 155-

The ones possessing total awareness,
Are only known by others of total awareness.
For the exact weight of the earth,
Is only known to them.

verse 156-

If people let their virtues speak through their actions,
Even those who do not have virtues will acquire them.
But the one who boast of his virtues,
Even if a wise man, would not be respected.

verse 157-

Where being wise and honest is not respected,
Then why would the wise and honest go?
In such a place as that,
What would the wise and honest do?

verse 158-

It is the ignorant that mimic each other,
For they are incapable of personal thinking.
By imitating each other,
They remain in the darkness.

verse 159-

The idiot admires the clever man.
For he considers him to be superior.
The idiot and the clever man acquire wealth,
While the wise goes empty handed.

verse 160-

As the sage passes time with various acts of virtue,
He notices not his state of indigence.
While this extreme poverty seems suffering,
To the sage it is not hardship, it is the joy from within.

verse 161-

One who makes company with many people,
Spending his days at the market,
And yet chooses not to obtain the virtues of the holy,
Then what is his profit in being born?

verse 162-

The way of the wise man is knowledge,
The way of the cuckoo is a sweet note,
The way of the ascetic is patience,
The way of a woman is perversity.

verse 163-

Astronomy itself and doctrinal principles,
The Eagle-spell and the repeating of spells,
(Of these) the essential meaning should be seized.
Do not analyze the sound of the words.

verse 164-

Knowledge that is left in books,
Wealth that is taken from others,
When the time comes that both are needed,
Neither will be there

verse 165-

The teacher of the arts has many accomplishments.
But these accomplishments come from earning a living,
But the study of the termination of earthly incarnation,
Why should that not be the only accomplishment?

verse 166-

With great care and thought be made,
Before giving sound advice to a man.
For like giving pearls to a monkey.
It will soon be cast to the ground

verse 167-

Some spend countless hours preaching,
Some attain their desire without speaking.
The reed-flower has no fruit,
The walnut has both flower and fruit.

verse 168-

The nut of the Kataka tree purifies water,
By immersing it into the muddy waters.
If not immersed but only mentioned,
Does the muddy water become clear?

verse 169-

A man that possesses knowledge of the written word,
And yet he does not apply what he has learned,
Is like a blind man carrying a lamp during the day,
He is still unable to see the road.

verse 170-

Like the moon which waxes and wanes,
Shines equally on the holy and the ignorant.
While you may attain a little virtue,
You may also lose vast accomplishments.

verse 171-

It is far easier to have a clever man for one's enemy,
Than to be friends with the unlearned and ignorant.
For it is better to have a worthy opponent you know,
Then to battle a monkey or a cow.

verse 172-

The clever, the disciplined,
The contented and the tellers of truth,
It is better for such to die,
Than to live in the kingdom of the evil.

verse 173-

What is more deadly, a snake's venom or that of an evil man?
An evil man is more venomous than a snake,
For the snake's venom may be overcome by drugs.
But what can soothe the venom of an evil man?

verse 174-

Although the evil may be benefited by fortune and gain.
Yet, even when happy, they still use abusive language.
He who is well educated and steadfast is firm.
Although poor and penniless, he will not abandon virtue.

verse 175-

The naturally evil man,
Is like the beam and balance scales.
A little thing sends him up,
And a little thing brings him down.

verse 176-

Although smeared with sandalwood, musk and camphor,
The natural strong smell of garlic is not driven out.
Although one may study very well the many texts,
One does not drive out the natural evil in one's disposition.

verse 177-

As there are no markings on the son of a holy man.
There are no markings on the son of a prostitute.
But the perversion of the act is evident by the presence,
And is the essential characteristic of the bastard.

verse 178-

The word which is uttered is one thing,
And different from the thought in the mind.
This is the way of the crooked-minded,
Who can change his natural disposition?

verse 179-

He firmly with resolve retains his vices,
While he continues to discard moral virtues.
In retaining vice and discarding virtue,
The evil man resembles a strainer.

verse 180-

He who has been falsely accused by an evil man,
Loses confidence even in the holy and wise.
Like a child's mouth has been scalded by hot milk,
He will blow even on cold milk before drinking it.

verse 181-

Seeing the stars' reflection on the lake by night,
The swan is disappointed in taking them for lotus shoots,
Even when he sees the real lotus shoot by day he will not eat it.
When once refuted by a liar, one will doubt even the truthful.

verse 182-

Twice as much as a man, a woman's appetite.
Four times as much, her deceitfulness.
Six times as much, her shame.
Eight times as much, her passion, so it is said.

verse 183-

Not by giving gifts or attention.
Not by worship or veneration.
Not by constant association.
None of these will control a woman.

verse 184-

When he was carried off by the King of the Birds,
The White Lotus Serpent God said:
He who tells secrets to women,
His life is lost there and then.

verse 185-

By committing adultery, they destroy the others faith,
In their object of desire and religion,
Causing much suffering this creates an obstacle to salvation.
Therefore avoid the wife of another man.

verse 186-

If even one written verse of truth,
Is given by a Lama to his pupil,
The gift given would be supreme.
Such a thing is not on earth.

verse 187-

All worldly pleasures should be abandoned,
But, if you are unable to abandon them,
Then cling to the holy with all your might.
As this is the cure for it.

verse 188-

All desires should be abandoned,
But if you cannot abandon them,
Let your desires be for salvation.
As this is the cure for it.

verse 189-

The unhelpful brother is like a stranger,
But he who helps, even if he is an outsider, is a brother.
Like the body and its diseases which are with us,
Solitude is the beneficial medicine of the soul.

verse 190-

If you hold a pot full of water over your head,
With persistence and diligence,
So it is as with respect,
The evil man becomes angry and excited.

verse 191-

Whatever may be agreeable to your mind,
Although it is far away, it is too, very near.
That which is not kept firmly planted in your mind,
Although it may be your side, it is too, very far.

verse 192-

Though we may live in the society of the wicked
There is no intimacy like the water and the lotus.
The holy may ever live far apart,
Yet they rejoice like the moon and the water-lily.

verse 193-

If you desire true friendship,
Then avoid the following,
Gambling , the lending and borrowing of money,
And speaking lustily with women.

verse 194-

When milk flows from the bees,
When honey flows from a cow,
Then, when a woman is true,
The lotus will grow in dry ground.

verse 195-

A man possessed of very little moral merit,
Even though he obtains abundance, knows not how to enjoy it,
Like a dog on a frozen lake, which, when thirsty
Licks the ice with its tongue, receives no satisfaction.

verse 196-

Those who do work in this world,
Would not work without profit
But beggars and the poor, without its being evident.
Have a hundredfold profit in the future.

verse 197-

It is natural that we will all die one day
Leaving our wealth behind, therefore give it away while alive.
When you die your property is not lost,
Realize that giving alms is like the act of a clever miser.

verse 198-

The miserable do not give alms,
For they fear they may become impoverished.
But wealth is the real danger,
Knowing this, the learned man distributes his wealth.

verse 199-

Why not give about half of your food to the beggars?
Charity brings rewards back to you tenfold.
While you may not see the immediate rewards,
It will be obtained at some time.

verse 200-

Even though you may not see results from your actions,
Do not be grieved by this, or feel sorrow.
You can still give alms from your possessions.
Be dedicated in your resolve to give as it is honorable.

verse 201-

Wealth is devoid of charity and enjoyment.
Such an owner of wealth in living in error.
Even though it is your property, why not use it,
Either in giving it away or to be enjoyed.

verse 202-

You are placed here on earth for action.
Your results here go to the beyond.
Whatever actions you may do here,
The same will certainly be enjoyed there.

verse 203-

Be envious not for wealth, rank, beauty, and health.
For these are not to be grieved for.
If you desire these, then practice virtuous action.
Like the fruits of a tree came from one time, a seed.

verse 204-

If you hoard your possessions and do not distribute them,
Then what is the use of having them?
Like the fruits of the Horse-apple tree,
While bountiful, what is its use in hunger?

verse 205-

The pleasure in giving alms which do not harm others,
Is a gift that cannot be carried away by water,
Nor burnt by fire or stolen by thieves,
Such possessions will never be utterly destroyed.

verse 206-

He that does not strive for salvation from Hell,
What will he do once he reaches that place?
When no medicine exists for his disease,
What will he do other than die?

verse 207-

Holy men are seized by the snake of words,
Which comes from the pit of savage men.
As a means of a cure from this poison,
Drink the medicine of wisdom and patience.

verse 208-

Although you may kill many during your life,
You will not reduce the number of your enemies.
But if your own anger be slain,
That is to slay the real enemy.

verse 209-

The mighty are not easy to reform,
Therefore why exercise patience with them.
Those who are disciplined and peaceful in conduct
What necessity is there for patience?

verse 210-

If you are merely angry owing to a grudge,
Then why not be angry with the anger?
Which obviously destroys religious aims,
For salvation, one must let go of anger.

verse 211-

He who having seen the excellence of others,
Is afflicted by envy or jealousy in his own mind,
Will not gain even a little of the Truth.
Such a being destroys his own merit.

verse 212-

Let all hear this moral maxim,
And having heard it keep it well:
Whatever is not pleasing to yourself,
Do not do that unto others.

verse 213-

In regards to leaving this mortal life,
Who is not clever in knowing and speaking about it?
But when it comes to practicing what they preach
Those who do would be considered wise among the sages.

verse 214-

The conduct of mankind is very surprising!
Youth perishes with age and property is unsecured.
Life is constantly being stalked by Death.
Yet mankind clings to this life, refusing to let go.

verse 215-

He who possesses intellect but is lazy,
Will never but held in high esteem.
Like a child who writes in the dust,
His works never last.

verse 216-

If people, all of them,
Could only perceive Death on their own heads
Even in food there would be no flavor or pleasure.
Not to mention other things

verse 217-

Death does not wait to ask whether,
Your works are completed or not.
Therefore do tomorrow's work today,
And the evening's work in the morning.

verse 218-

As long as you are healthy and produce a harvest,
That is not ruined by the great hail of disease,
As long as your intellect is in your work,
This is the time for adhering to religious doctrines.

verse 219-

What are strings of pearls to donkeys and cattle?
What is delicate food to dogs and pigs?
Light to the blind or songs to the deaf?
Of what use is religious doctrine to fools?

verse 220-

Strive to have your accomplishments serve others,
Rather than have them serve your ego.
If ego rules your actions,
Then how are morals attained?

verse 221-

Strive not to be a beggar, even if the times demand it.
Strive to live that of a glorious ascetic.
Be brave, clever, that of high rank.
Manly are these traits until you beg.

verse 222-

The first to accomplish a difficult task,
Is considered a hero.
However, in regards to building a fire,
It can even be done by a child.

verse 223-

A sage's son may conveniently die soon,
And a king's son may conveniently live for a long time.
For the hunter's son life and death are equally unsuitable,
For the saint's son equally convenient.

verse 224-

Let that which exists in the beginning,
continue to exist,
For the purpose of increasing man's
understanding of them.
Let the elegant classics be expounded and
learned,
By the man who understands these doctrines.

verse 225-

The words of elegant sayings,
Should be collected as a convenience.
For the temporary but supreme gift of words,
Any price will be paid.

verse 226-

The student of science, the hero,
And every beautifully formed woman,
Wherever they go,
Acquire great fame, there and then.

verse 227-

A scientist and a king,
Are not to be compared in any way.
The king is esteemed in his own country.
The wise man is esteemed wherever he goes.

verse 228-

He may be handsome, youthful, accomplished,
And born of high caste, yet,
Like a new born hawk or owl ,
Does not look well when removed from his nest.

verse 229-

He who has a body but is ignorant of knowledge,
Even though of good birth, what use is he?
In the world respect comes from knowledge.
From lack of knowledge comes destruction.

verse 230-

If you desire an easy life, give up learning.
If you desire learning, give up ease.
How can the man at his ease acquire knowledge,
And how can the earnest student enjoy ease?

verse 231-

He who is ignorant of knowledge,
Will always be in misery and pain.
He who is wise in knowledge,
Will always obtain joy and happiness.

verse 232-

What country is foreign to a sage?
Who is hostile to a pleasant speaker?
What load is heavy to a man in his own home?
What distance is long to the energetic?

verse 233-

Since he who is unselfish, has many friends,
The summit of the king of mountains is not too high,
The earth's depth of intellect is not too deep,
And even when torn apart by the ocean it is not beyond his reach.

verse 234-

The superior man who has learned from only books,
And has not studied from many different perspectives,
Is like a pregnant girl of loose morals.
He does not look well at a gathering.

verse 235-

The one that scorns the teaching of a Lama,
Even if only a single letter,
Will pass through a hundred incarnations,
As a dog and be reborn of low caste.

verse 236-

A single grain of wisdom bestowed upon you,
By a Lama as you are the pupil,
That is a debt that if paid by you,
Cannot be sufficiently paid in full.

verse 237-

He who brings one up, he who teaches the way,
He who teaches him science,
Who feeds one and gives the gift of fearlessness,
These five are declared to be like fathers.

verse 238-

The wife of a king or of a minister,
Likewise the wife of a friend,
A brother's wife, and one's own mother,
These five are be treated like mothers.

verse 239-

Giving advice to a fool,
While it may excite him,
It is still like giving your pearls,
To the dogs and pigs.

verse 240-

The fool is nothing more an inanimate beast.
You should especially avoid them.
Like stepping on an unseen thorn,
The pain of their words hurts.

verse 241-

When a fool sees another fool,
He is overcome with joy.
If he sees a learned man,
He regards him as a murderer.

verse 242-

The evil are not grateful towards you,
For any benefit that is given to them.
However even the smallest act towards a holy man,
Will give you command of him for life.

verse 243-

The actions of a fool are like a stone thrown into the pond,
Quickly will the ripples fade away.
The actions of a holy man are like a carving on stone,
They may be small but they are permanent.

verse 244-

Even though the evil man may speak sweetly,
He is not to be trusted at any moment.
Like the peacock that has beautiful plumage,
It devours and consumes all in its path.

verse 245-

The evil man and phlegm are really alike.
By mildness they are both excited,
And require attention but,
By roughness they are both dealt with.

verse 246-

These are controlled by beating,
An evil man, gold, a drum,
A wild horse, and cloth
These are not the means for elegant doings.

verse 247-

Association with the evil man is not appropriate,
Whether he is pleasant or obnoxious.
As with a dog, it's not appropriate,
Whether you play with him or let him lick you.

verse 248-

Reckless abandonment is worse than a snake.
A snake's venom can be cured by drugs,
But committing reckless abandonment,
Cannot be cured by anything.

verse 249-

The sins of the unruly and undisciplined,
Leave their mark on the temperament.
Like stepping into fresh cow dung,
Surely you too will carry the smell with you.

verse 250-

Even without noticing his father's conduct,
The son imitates him.
From the Pecan tree,
One does not get oranges.

verse 251-

If my father, my mother, own my brother,
And my wife copies me and my actions,
In whatever sin I commit,
It is as if they had committed it too.

verse 252-

This earth, the mighty ocean,
And the mountains are not a burden,
But he who is ungrateful towards nature,
Is indeed a heavy burden to mother earth.

verse 253-

He who stays in the society of those of the Way,
And is full of compassion and love for his enemies.
Although he may be destroyed by them,
Wise men will praise him very much.

verse 254-

In the society of the clever, the disciplined,
The contented, and the truthful,
Imprisonment is a superior state over,
The sovereignty of the unruly.

verse 255-

Immersing into the society of the holy.
Associate within the society of the learned.
Be among the unselfish.
These actions will not cause any regrets.

verse 256-

Perhaps for a very long time you've not perceived the misery,
Caused by your sins in this world and in the other world,
Strive still to bring your mind into the harmony of the way,
So you may live in the divine love of the Way.

verse 257-

Although you may enjoy a thing.
Yet, if given in fullness would cause bodily harm,
And upsets your health,
How could such a thing be right to consume?

verse 258-

That is which is painful but required for profit.
Like that of a bitter medicine to be cured.
The results attained afterwards,
In themselves will be incomparable.

verse 259-

If a learned king can grasp the meaning of these verses,
From the beginning, to the middle and to the end,
And if he realizes that it is as it is written,
He will then be in possession of wisdom.

verse 260-

When the ocean shall be no more.
It may be crossed in the middle, so they say.
Whether holy men exist or not,
We should never abandon the moral codes.

End of the translation

CHAPTER FOUR
CONVICTION OF THE HEART

"Where are the dreams that we once had? Where are the promises that we once made? Are they lost and forgotten or still on the tip of our tongue? When did we all become so bogged down with life that we lost our way? When did the voice become silent within? When did we forget and become lost on the path of life? When did we become separated from it all?"

Living an authentic life is something that requires attention on a daily basis. The method I used is to ask myself three simple questions every day. One, did I matter today? Did I make a difference? and lastly, Did I love today?

How can I matter or make a difference? It is in the simple things that lay greatness. For instance, an act as simple as acknowledging someone can have a profound effect. An example, I go through the toll booth just about every day at the airport. When I do, I'll say in a big way, "How is my favorite DFW kind of guy doing today?" Well, the first few times, they think I'm crazy.

But what is interesting is after a few times, when I pull up to their booth, they have a big smile, sometimes they tell me they missed me the day before. Do you see what is happening here? These are the people that are discarded and ignored by people in a hurry to get out of the nightmare that DFW Airport is and get home.

By acknowledging them, you bring a little happiness into their world, giving them something to look forward to, a little brightness on an otherwise dreary day. That my friend is making a difference in someone's life and that matters.

On love, I have visited with several people on their death bed and not one time did I ever hear, "I wished I would have bought Apple at $34.00" or "I wish I would have worked more overtime." No! What I hear is how they wished they would have spent more time with their loved ones, more time doing what it was *that made them happy.*

And for those who worked their entire life so "Someday" they could have the life they wanted are the ones that had the biggest regrets. You see, "Someday Isle" is no place to go to. Oh, it has a sister, and it's called, "One Day Isle. " Neither one offers true peace or happiness. There is only one place that matters and that is "Now." Learn to forget about some day and start living in the now.

In the now is where everything you want and need lives. Peace and happiness is in the now. Regret and depression are the past. Anxiety and worry are the future, but in the now, there is only peace.

Find whatever works for you and stick with it. The rewards are beyond what you can imagine.

Here is a thought from George Carlin-

"Let's take an inventory, We have taller buildings but shorter tempers; wider freeways but narrower viewpoints.

We spend more but have less; we buy more but enjoy less.

We have bigger houses and smaller families; more conveniences but less time.

We have more degrees but less sense; more knowledge but less judgment; more experts yet more problems; more medicine but less wellness.

We drink too much, smoke too much, spend too recklessly, laugh too little, drive too fast, get too angry, stay up too late, get up too tired, read too little, watch TV too much, and pray too seldom.

We have multiplied our possessions but reduced our values.

We talk too much, love too seldom, and hate too often.

We've learned how to make a living but not a life.

We've added years to life, not life to years.

We've been all the way to the moon and back, but have trouble crossing the street to meet a new neighbor.

We've conquered outer space but not inner space.

We've done larger things but not better things.

We've cleaned up the air but polluted the soul.

We've conquered the atom but not our prejudice.

We write more but learn less.

We plan more but accomplish less.

We've learned to rush but not to wait.

These are the times of fast food and slow digestion, big men and small characters, steep profits and shallow relationships.

These are the days of two incomes but more divorce; fancier houses but broken homes.

These are the days of quick trips, disposable diapers, throwaway morality, one night stands, overweight bodies, and pills that do everything from cheer to quiet to kill.

It is a time when there is much in the showroom window and nothing in the stockroom."

What does it avail a man if he gains the world and loses his soul?

Where are those Dreams? Where are those promises that we made? It's time to bring them back my friend, it's time.

There is a whole new world out there waiting for you and me. It is time to stop living life through the mind and start living life through the heart. It is time to forgive and forget. It is time to believe. It is time to be healed. It is time to take action. It is time for us to find that inner voice within us all and listen to it, for it has been waiting for us. It is time to live with conviction of the heart.

If you are at a crossroad in life, troubled with which way to go, listen to your heart. What is your heart telling you? What are you feeling? The bottom-line to any decision you make in life should be to honor and follow your heart.

You're never too old to start over, never too old to dream again, never too old to rekindle your love and passion. Your heart is timeless and lives in eternity. Your heart can and will guide you to the right path. But only if you listen to it.

There is only one chance to live this one life. It's never too late. Never too late to believe. As for me, I'm tired of thinking that I loved, thinking that I am doing the right thing, I'm tired of fooling myself that this life is all there is and nothing more.

How long must we wait to change? It's time to break free from these chains and start living life with a conviction of the heart. It is time to love with a conviction of the heart. It is time to start looking at life with a conviction of the heart. It's time for a conviction of the heart.

With a conviction of heart, you'll spend more time with your loved ones, because they are not going to be around forever. You'll say a kind word to someone who looks up to you in awe, because that little person will soon grow up and leave your side. You'll give a warm hug to the one next to you, because that is the only treasure you can give with your heart and it doesn't cost a cent. You'll say "I love you" to your partner and your loved ones, but most of all mean it. You'll know that a kiss and an embrace will mend the hurt, especially when it comes from deep inside of your heart. You'll hold hands and cherish the moments with loved ones, friends and family, for someday those people will not be here. Give and make time to love! Give time to speak! And give time to share the precious thoughts in your mind.

Life is not measured by the number of breaths we take, but by the moments that take our breath away. Yes George, you were so right!

Living with a conviction of the heart will renew your passion for life. With renewed passion you'll take action to live the life that is meant for you. You'll see in this world that everyone you meet is a part of you and you a part of them. Hurt, anger, agony, pain, jealously, envy, they will all slip away.

There will be no need of these negative emotions anymore in your life. You'll see that the only thing that truly matters in this world is love. A universal unconditional love. With conviction of the heart you'll strive to live in joy, peace and happiness. Living a life with conviction of the heart, you'll become like your heart, one with the earth, one with the sky, and like your heart, timeless, living in the eternity while being in the now.

Through my heart I see that we are One, that everything is One. We are all just different facets on the Jewel. While all of us are looking at life from a different perspective, if we would only look inward, we would all be seeing the same thing, each other. In that view, we would realize these simple truths. That hurting you is hurting me. I know through my heart that forgiving you is forgiving me. In letting go of the pain, by letting go of the past, by living through the heart, I find peace.

There is Peace when living with a conviction of the heart. There is no depression in the now, only in the past. There is no anxiety in the now. Only in thinking about the future is there anxiety. There is Peace when we live in the now. And we live with a conviction of the heart, we are always in the now surrounded by divine love.

There is only one us, only one earth, one sky, one world. There is only now. And it is time now to start living with a conviction of the heart. It is time to take action. Because this is all we have, is this "now."

There is only one thing that you should Never give up on. Only one thing that you should Never compromise on, and that is Love. The Love that comes from living with a conviction of the heart.

"Inspired by Kenny Loggins and George Carlin"

ABOUT THE AUTHOR

Dennis Waller, author of several books, is recognized as an expert on spiritual experience, self-discovery, and exploring the human consciousness. As a writer, speaker and philosopher, his teachings invoke an introspective view on how to discover one's true authentic self through a higher sense of consciousness and awareness. He teaches classes in the Dallas area on several subjects including Enochian Magic and Developing Your Psychic Abilities. He is best known for his work in the field of Indigos, people who possess unusual or supernatural abilities. His other fields of expertise include comparative religion, the law of attraction, and interpreting Eastern thought's relevancy to science and quantum physics. He is in demand as a guest speaker on radio programs, a lecturer at churches and life enrichment groups, and conducts workshops for Indigos.

He doesn't like long walks on the beach at night unless it is with the love of his life nor does he care for round colorful balloons but he does enjoy an occasional game of cricket on a sunny spring day. This bit of non-sense is included to see if you really read these bios. If you have then you will enjoy his sense of humor. Never take life too seriously, you will die someday so make the most of it, go out for an ice-cream, feed the ducks and tell someone you love that you do love them, even if they're mad at you, unless they're really really mad like someone I know, (hint hint), then, just maybe a phone call would be better.

Now, enough with the non-sense, but really, find a way to enjoy live and love!

For more information on Dennis Waller, please go to www.amazon.com/DennisWaller/e/B009HBKD8M

Here is a partial list of other books by Dennis Waller

The Way of the Tao- Living an Authentic Life

The Tao of Kenny Loggins

The Importance of the Tao- A Short Essay

Zen and Tao- A Little Book on Buddhist Thought and Meditation

Hsin Hsin Ming

Nagarjuna's Tree of Wisdom- A Translation

Are You an Indigo- Discover Your Authentic Self

Indigo Wisdom- with Francesca Rivera

The Art of Talking to Christ- The Theory and Practices of Christian Mysticism

You may contact Dennis at
dennismwaller@yahoo.com

NOTES

NOTES

NOTES

NOTES

Made in United States
Troutdale, OR
09/09/2025